D1536094

ALL BUENOS AIRES

Text: Mario Sergio Banchik and Diego A. del Pino
Photographs: Mario Banchik, Oscar Flores and Miriam Schvemer

Reproduction and layout produced and designed entirely by
the technical team of EDITORIAL ESCUDO DE ORO, S.A.

Rights of reproduction and translation
(in whole or in part) reserved.

Copyright of this edition applies to photographs and text:
© EDITORIAL ESCUDO DE ORO, S.A.
Palaudàries, 26 - 08004 Barcelona (Spain)
© EDICIONES TURÍSTICAS, S.A.
Av. Belgrano, 3027 - (C1209AAC) Buenos Aires (Argentina)

Editorial Escudo de Oro, S.A.

National and city flags.

INTRODUCTION

Buenos Aires is the capital city of the Republic of Argentina, a country in the south of the American continent. Its territory extends over 3,700,000 km², and it has a population of 37,000,000. 80% of its inhabitants are of European descent, a result of the great waves of immigrants arriving from the middle of the 19th Century onwards. The national language is Spanish, with slight variations in each of its regions. Most of its inhabitants profess to be Roman Catholic, but there is in fact complete freedom of worship with churches of many creeds, as might be expected in a country with an open immigration policy, receiving «all men of good will», as its National Constitution puts it. Its government is democratic, republican and federal, with a President as head of its Executive Power, Legislative Power consisting of two Chambers (of Senators and Deputies), and an independent Judicial power. Due to its geographical situation, Argentina's regions are very diverse in nature, and have varied climates: the plain or pampa, in the centre of the country, formerly the stamping ground of the legendary «gauchos»; in the west high mountains, the Andes Range, the highest of which is the Aconcagua, at its almost 7,000 metres; steep tablelands in Patagonia in the south; mountain ranges in the centre and north-west; rivers, woodlands and fertile ground in the north-east. Not forgetting the majestic Waterfalls of Iguazú, the impressive gullies of the Perito Moreno Glacier and the fascinating fauna of the Valdés Peninsula, all of which have been declared World Heritage Sites by UNESCO.

Buenos Aires is in the mid-east of the country, on the River Plate, «one of the widest in the world» it is claimed, although it is really a 220 km wide fresh water, terracotta-coloured estuary.

BUENOS AIRES

The Argentine capital is a cosmopolitan city that strikingly recalls Europe in its architecture, with grand avenues, a vertiginous lifestyle and a dizzying choice of culture, art and after-dark entertainment. In it live more than three million souls, and if we also include the residents of «Greater Buenos Aires», this total rises to more than seven million. It covers an area of 200 km², and its outer limit is marked by a road that runs round its perimeter, the Avenida General Paz. Its climate is temperate, its winters are not very severe –it never snows– with temperatures of between 5° and 17° C. Summer is rather more extreme and it can reach 25 to 35 degrees. There are never more than four or five rainy days on average per month, with a total annual rainfall of 900 mm. Buenos Aires has an extensive underground and surface transport network, many bus routes covering the whole of the city and its surrounding area, short and long haul train services, a large number of taxis and two airports, one for national and regional services and another, 30 minutes away outside the city, for international flights. The last ten years have seen the designing of modern motorways that have considerably speeded up the complicated traffic in this great metropolis.

Avenida Nueve de Julio.

Old view of the city from the River Plate.

History

The city was first founded in 1536 by the Spanish conquistador Pedro de Mendoza, on a site near to the present-day Lezama Park, in the south. This settlement did not last long, given the scarcity of food and attacks by the indigenous people –Querandí Indians– who lived in the region, and it was abandoned within a few years. Later, in 1580, a fresh expedition led by Juan de Garay set sail from the old city of Asunción in Paraguay, to found the city for a second time on the «Mouth of the Waters» or the «Doors of the Earth» as the River Plate was known. The place he chose was what has now become the Plaza de Mayo. In the plains encircling the new township the livestock abandoned by the Spanish after the first expedition had multiplied, and it was these enormous herds that provided the settlement with its early wealth. Garay awarded the settlers or «vecinos» (neighbours) as they were then known, land in one of three categories: the first was land near the Plaza Mayor; the second and larger category, land known as «chacras» (smallholdings), further from the centre of the city; and the third and even larger category, lands known as «estancias» (ranches), starting where the chacras left off. The name given to the city at that time was «Most Holy Trinity and Port of Santa Maria of the Good Winds». During these early days the «city» was in fact just a village. Its houses were built of clay bricks since there was no stone in the area. Roofs were first made of straw, and later of Spanish-type tiles. The houses themselves were laid out in squares forming a grid. The city gradually began to prosper, and when in 1776 the River Plate Vice-Royalty was formed, its population took an upturn and its trading activity increased. On 25 May 1810 a revolutionary movement started up, aiming to achieve separation from Spain, although this only became a reality in 1816. The National Constitution of 1853 abolished slavery and brought political order to the country. Buenos Aires started to assume greater importance, and in 1880 was declared Federal Capital. From that time on a massive influx of immigrants began, mostly Italians and Spanish, although also including many other nationalities, and the city began to expand. Its transport systems –railways (1857) and trams (1863)– made it possible to form new centres of population or «barrios» (districts). From 1890 on, buildings changed first to an Italian and then, with the coming in of the 20th Century, to a typical French style of architecture. Splendid palaces were built, many of which can still be admired today.

Old view of the Plaza de Mayo.

Couples dancing the Tango.

THE TANGO

The tango is the music of Buenos Aires: nowadays it has also become popularly identified throughout the world as the music of Argentina in general. Its melodies, words and dance have in recent years served as ambassadors for the national culture. Not much is known about the origin of the tango, but several theories define it as a mixture of African sounds and Andalusian tunes. All we know for sure is that it originated at the end of the 19th Century as the musical expression of the mar-

Plazoleta del Tango.

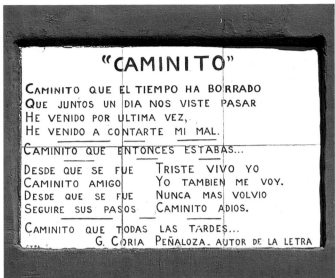

"CAMINITO"

CAMINITO QUE EL TIEMPO HA BORRADO
QUE JUNTOS UN DIA NOS VISTE PASAR
HE VENIDO POR ULTIMA VEZ,
HE VENIDO A CONTARTE MI MAL.

CAMINITO QUE ENTONCES ESTABAS...

DESDE QUE SE FUE   TRISTE VIVO YO
CAMINITO AMIGO   YO TAMBIEN ME VOY.
DESDE QUE SE FUE   NUNCA MAS VOLVIO
SEGUIRE SUS PASOS   CAMINITO ADIOS.

CAMINITO QUE TODAS LAS TARDES...
        G. CORIA PEÑALOZA, AUTOR DE LA LETRA

Details of El Viejo Almacén, where tango shows are held, reproduction of the tango «Caminito» somewhere in the city and shop window with typical tango instruments (with victrola and bandoneón) and a portrait of Carlos Gardel.

María Eva Duarte de Perón, «Evita».

ginal populations living on the outskirts of the city. Little by little, its melancholy tunes, romantic words with their intense social content and sensual choreography gained in popularity, until it was even accepted by the upper classes and in the best-known haunts of the city's nightlife. Curiously, all this happened during the 1920's, when the tango arrived in Paris and carried all before it. It returned to Buenos Aires as music that «had been accepted in Europe». The instruments first used in the tango were the guitar, the viola and the flute, joined later by the «bandoneón», an instrument of German origin similar to an accordion, which came to be both synonymous with and a symbol of the tango. The choreography of the tango invites a bodily contact between the male and female partners that often borders on the indecent. Aesthetically beautiful, it requires close co-ordination and a lot of hard work from its practitioners.

To name here the host of orchestras, singers and dancers that have contributed to transforming this music into a cultural movement would be impossible. It is enough just to mention its most famous exponent: Carlos Gardel.

Today the tango is undergoing a revival throughout the country, with many academies springing up to teach its techniques. Shows, dance halls and its tunes themselves have helped it take the world by storm, particularly in some Eastern and European countries and in North America.

PERSONALITIES

The city has been the cradle of personalities whose standing has earned them worldwide recognition. Although engaged in very different fields of activity, these have all been or are now representatives of Buenos Aires and of their country. Between 1915 and 1935, the figure of Carlos Gardel was known all over the world. Today, Gardel is a «porteño» (Buenos Aires) idol, his death in a flying accident over Colombia transforming him into a myth.

The 1950's were dominated by the woman who was the wife of the then-president of the Republic, María Eva Duarte de Perón. Her dedication to improving the lot of the lowest social classes and her prema-

Two examples of Argentine cuisine: asado criollo and the typical gourds in which mate tea is taken.

ture death converted her into the «champion of the needy». Curiously, her personality has been further promoted by the English «rock opera» that bears her name, and by other films that have gone towards making «Evita» almost a legend.

During the 1960's, the racing driver Juan Manuel Fangio came to international prominence when he won five world championships.

Another internationally renowned character is the footballer, Diego Armando Maradona. For several years, his skill and his quality as a professional earned him the place of the world's top football player.

Any such list would be incomplete if it left out that outstanding man of letters, Jorge Luis Borges. The fact that he was never awarded the Nobel Prize for Literature in no way detracts from the magnificent quality of his prose, his poetry, his wide-ranging culture and his expertise in the more exotic literatures. These days, in the majority of the world's Universities, he is studied, analysed, admired and permanent source of inspiration for new works of criticism.

Also worthy of a place of honour are Carlos Saavedra Lamas (Nobel Prize for Peace in 1936), Bernardo A. Houssay (Nobel Prize for Medicine and Physiology in 1947), Luis Federico Leloir (Nobel Prize for Chemistry in 1970), Adolfo Pérez Esquivel (Nobel Prize for Peace in 1980) and Cesar Milstein (Nobel Prize for Medicine in 1984).

GASTRONOMY

Argentina is famous for the excellent quality of its beef. Although there is no dish identified traditionally and exclusively with the city of Buenos Aires, it could be said that «bife de chorizo» (a charcoal-grilled slice of beef approximately 3 or 4 centimetres thick) is the city's most typical fare. Also very common in the city, although found in other regions of the country as well, are products such as «dulce de leche» (a paste produced by reducing milk with sugar until it turns dark brown), mate (an infusion of the leaves and stalks of a plant called «yerbamate», that Argentinians consume in small, dried, hollowed-out gourds, sipping the liquid with a «bombilla» (a tube or drinking straw), and «asado criollo» (beef and lamb cooked over a hot grill). Also worthy of note are the country's excellent wines.

But Buenos Aires, like any cosmopolitan city with immigrants from many lands, has a rich cuisine: ranging through fast food, traditional restaurants of countries all over the world, and luxurious venues with their exquisite fare. This is a city where you can eat whenever you want –many restaurants are open virtually day and night– although «porteños» themselves like to lunch between 1 p.m. and 3 p.m. and have dinner between 9 and 12 midnight.

The Obelisk.

THE CENTRE OF BUENOS AIRES

Although the city is divided into 47 «barrios» or districts, for the purposes of a tour around it three main regions or directions can be distinguished: the Centre, commercial, political and recreational hub of the city; the North, the residential area, including many parks and museums; and lastly, the South, the historical city with its port and many traditions.

It is a good idea to set off from one of the city's most emblematic monuments. **The Obelisk,** inaugurated in 1936, is a solid structure 67 meters in height, constructed as part of the events commemorating the 400th anniversary of the city's first foundation. The square around it is the **Plaza de la República**, formed by two green semi-circles in which the shields of each of the country's provinces are exhibited. Perhaps the most interesting fact is that both the square and the Obelisk are right at the intersection of one of most important of the city's through-roads, **Avenida Nueve de Julio**, with the **Avenida Corrientes,** one of its most traditional streets and well-known all over the world.

Avenida Nueve de Julio is proudly proclaimed to be «the widest in the world». In fact, it measures 140 metres, and its widening meant the demolishing of a line of «manzanas» (blocks of land that make up the city) right along its length before it could be re-opened in 1937. These days it is one of the city's most important traffic thoroughfares, uniting the rapid throughways that run out towards the north and south of the city. This imposing setting provides a framework for many beautiful buildings, fountains, sculptures and monuments. And along it are to be found the offices of important companies and government institutions, hotels, cinemas, theatres and shops.

Avenida Corrientes has strong sentimental associations both for inhabitants of the city and for its visitors. First planned in 1820, it was originally just a narrow pathway running westwards. It rose

Details of the Plaza de la Republica: the shields of the country's various provinces.

Aerial view of Avenida Nueve de Julio and the Obelisk (by courtesy of Diario La Nación).

Avenida Nueve de Julio.

to fame a century later when it came to house the majority of the city's night-time entertainments –cinemas, cafés, theatres and bookshops– and gained its nickname of «the street that never sleeps». This name is commemorated in many tangos, where it is referred to for decades as the centre of city life. It was widened around 1940, when it took on the appearance it has today. Running down the entire length of this street is the **«Línea B» underground train**, taking you right to the end of the avenue, the site of the **Chacarita cemetery,** the largest in the city. This cemetery is the resting place of such figures as Juan Domingo

Avenida Corrientes.

Aerial view of Avenida Nueve de Julio with the diagonal streets running across it (by courtesy of Diario La Nación).

Chacarita Cemetery: access gate.

Chacarita Cemetery: commemortive plaques on the tombs of Juan Domingo Perón and Carlos Gardel.

Perón, Carlos Gardel, Jorge Newbery, Alfonsina Storni, Benito Quinquela Martín and Aníbal Troilo, to cite the names of only some of its many illustrious occupants.

Above Avenida Nueve de Julio and only a couple of blocks away from the Obelisk is the **Colón Theatre**. This impressive building is the largest musical theatre in South America, and one of the most beautiful and famous throughout the world. It occupies the site of the city's first railway station. Work on its incident-prone construction was begun by the architect Francisco Tamburini, continued by Víctor Meano and concluded by Julio Dormal. It was finally opened on 25 May 1908 with the staging of the opera «Aida» by Giuseppe Verdi.

After passing through its imposing iron porch we find ourselves in a grand vestibule richly ornamented with marble columns and flights of steps. The latter give access to the concert hall itself, built in the form of a horseshoe, with red velvet upholstered polychrome wooden boxes, and a gigantic crystal chandelier with more than 500 lights – most remarkably, its interior can accommodate an orchestra. The whole hall is topped by an impressive dome containing a fresco by the Argentine artist Raúl Soldi. The stage covers an area similar to that of the hall, and an immense

Colón Theatre: Avenida Nueve de Julio façade.

Colón Theatre: details of the Plaza General Lavalle façade.

velvet curtain separates the two areas. According to aficionados, the theatre's acoustics are almost perfect.

The Colón Theatre has four basement floors, with space for preparing scenery, artists' dressing rooms, dining rooms, and others given over to costumes, hairdressing and footwear. Also important are its schools, responsible for launching the majority of the country's great singers, musicians, set designers and dancers, amongst whom is Julio Bocca. Through this national monument have passed such prestigious figures as Pietro Mascagni, Igor Stravinsky, Arturo Toscanini, Ricardo Strauss, Enrico Carusso, María Callas, Luciano Pavarotti, Plácido Domingo, José Carreras and Montserrat Caballé.

Curiously, the theatre's main entrance is not in Avenida Nueve de Julio, but in Libertad Street, facing **Plaza General Lavalle**. This square bears the name of a soldier who was active during the civil war that led to the country's National Independence, and its centre bears a monument celebrating this event. The square provides a setting for several buildings of great beauty, important both for their architectural qualities and for their public functions.

Continuing on past Avenida Córdoba, at its intersection with Libertad Street, we find the **Cervantes National Theatre**. This was built on the initiative of the Spanish actors Fernando Díaz de Mendoza and María Guerrero by the architects Aranda and Repetto and inaugurated in 1921. Its façade is a reproduction of that of the University of Alcalá de Henares (birthplace of Miguel de Cervantes Saavedra) and its architecture has echoes of the Spanish Renaissance style. Brought in for use in its construction were ceramic tiles from Valencia, stone slabs from Tarragona, seating from Seville and carpets, drapes and «front curtain» from Madrid. The costs were more than the couple could meet, and so the then-Argentine President, Marcelo T. de Alvear, decreed that the theatre should be bought as part of national heritage. In 1961 it was destroyed in a fire, and the present

Details of the Plaza General Lavalle.

Cervantes Theatre.

theatre, completely rebuilt, has a stage 29 metres wide and 16 deep, with a turntable of 12 metres in diameter.

Through this theatre have passed actors and companies of the standing of María Guerrero, Fernando Díaz de Mendoza, Luisa Vehil, Margarita Xirgu, Enrique Muiño, Blanca Podestá and Elías Allippi, among others. As the National Theatre, the Cervantes is committed to the promotion of traditional works by Argentine and other South American dramatists, as well as productions on a grand scale that could not easily have been taken on by private enterprise.

Almost opposite it on the corner is the **Synagogue of the Jewish Community of Argentina**. This building, the work of the architect Norman, shows Romanesque and Byzantine features, and was inaugurated during the first decade of the 20th Century. Able to accommodate a congregation of a thousand, this is just one of the several places of worship of this community in the city.

Diagonally opposite this, still in the square, lies the imposing **Palace of the Tribunals**, seat of Argentina's Judicial Power. The project, work of the French architect Norberto Maillart, was inaugurated in 1910, although for various reasons not completed until 1942. Neo-Greco-Roman in style, with an imposing flight of stairs framed by pilasters and domes, giving access through a huge iron door to the hall itself, where placed on a high

Details of the Synagogue of the Jewish Community of the Republic of Argentina.

Palace of the Tribunals.

19

General San Martín Theatre and Cultural Centre.

pedestal is a sculpture representing Justice, work of the Argentine sculptor Rogelio Yrurtia. Crowning the upper part of the façade is a sculpture incorporating human figures and the Tablets of the Law. In this building of great solemnity sit the Supreme Court of Justice and several High Courts, as well as being the seat of the country's Judicial Power. Returning to Avenida Corrientes, at number 1,500 is the **General San Martín Cultural Centre**. Opened in 1961, this centre is the work of the architect Mario Roberto Álvarez. Entering the building from Avenida Corrientes, there are several rooms devoted to the theatre, cinematography, conferences, exhibitions and varied displays. The largest of these is the «Martín Coronado» room, accommodating 1,200 spectators and equipped with a revolving stage. Entering from Sarmiento Street

we find a large Conference Centre. With a wide range of rooms catering for up to several thousand participants, simultaneous translation facilities and several basement floors for vehicles, this was for many years the city's largest conference and events complex.

Between numbers 1,000 and 700 of this same street, and after again crossing the Plaza de la República towards the Obelisk, we come across a series of large theatre buildings. The most interesting of these is the **El Nacional Theatre** that after several years of disuse following a fire has recently been rebuilt and refurbished. This theatre and its fellow establishments the **Maipo**, the **Astros** and the **Tabarís**, were all venues for the so-called «Revista Porteña», a kind of vaudeville with rather spicy content, that were well-known in the city for

El Nacional Theatre, Gran Rex Cinema and Theatre and Opera Theatre.

Two views of Florida Street.

Galerías Pacífico, in Florida Street.

more than forty years. Almost directly opposite these stand the architecturally imposing **Opera Cinema and Theatre** and **Gran Rex Cinema and Theatre**, both with a large capacity and normally used as settings for recitals and musical shows.

As we reach number 600 we come across one of the city's two pedestrianised streets. **Florida Street** was one of the first city streets to be established, and in the colonial era among the few to be surfaced with stone. And so it was known for a time as: «stone street». When it was pedestrianised and improved some centuries later, excavations uncovered remains of the original stone base, and today vestiges of this can be seen at its intersection with Diagonal Norte. Florida is a Buenos Aires street *par excellence*, and was formerly lined

from end to end with grand residences; an elegant street in which the most important shops had their establishments. These days it joins Avenida de Mayo with Plaza San Martín, and contains the shops of many prestigious brands, a host of eating places, and two large shopping centres: **Galería Jardín** and **Galerías Pacífico**. Recently refurbished, these two centres, built in 1891, are proud possessors of a dome with important frescos by the Argentine artists Demetrio Urruchúa, Antonio Berni, Lino Eneas Spilimbergo, Carlos Castagnino and Antonio Comeiro.

At the end of Avenida Corrientes is a large complex known as **Luna Park**. This is the largest covered stadium in the city, and depending on the type of entertainment on offer, can accommodate

Luna Park.

an audience of between 10,000 and 15,000. Built on the initiative of businessmen Ismael Pace and José Lectoure, it occupies one whole «block». Although originally designed for boxing and other sporting events, at present Luna Park is used for every type of entertainment: live music, dance, political events and large musical comedies. It is the only facility in the city that can lay down an artificial ice rink, where the company «Holiday on Ice» puts on its spectacles.

Facing the back of Luna Park is the Post Office headquarters at **Palacio del Correo**. This imposing

Palacio del Correo.

General view of the Plaza de Mayo and detail of the headscarfs of the «Mothers of the Plaza de Mayo».

building, the city's first public building along the lines of the Beaux Arts tradition, was opened in 1928. With striking architecture in the French Neo-Classical style, it has seven floors and a basement. Its stairway, passing through its majestic frontage with its columns and mansard roofs, gives access to a sumptuous hall lined with exotic woods and rich marbles. Also of note is the exquisite décor of its functions room. Nowadays, the building holds the offices of «Correo Argentino», a private postal company handling the concession for this public service.

Plaza de Mayo and the Casa Rosada.

Pirámide de Mayo. ▷

From the Palacio del Correo and continuing along Avenida Leandro N. Alem, a side street leads us to the **Plaza de Mayo**. This is undoubtedly the historical and political centre of the city, where both the city and the country have lived through the great milestones and events of their history. When Juan de Garay founded «La Santísima Trinidad», literally the Most Holy Trinity, (as the city was formerly known) and the Puerto de Santa María de los Buenos Ayres, literally the Port of Santa Maria of the Good Winds, (a name in part maintained to the present day), he chose the site of what is now the Plaza de Mayo with this in mind. For Spanish laws decreed that when a new city was founded in «The Indies» an open space, to be known as the Plaza Mayor, would be allocated for civic, military and religious meetings and

also to serve as a market. This square, which has been known by several names, was for almost a century (between 1801 and 1883) divided by a building called «La Recova», used as a station for carts and the market.

Since the city's foundation, its main public buildings have been grouped around the Plaza de Mayo: the Fort (today the seat of the President of the Republic), the Chapter House (now a Museum) and the Church (currently Buenos Aires' Cathedral). The square has been the stopping place for carriages, had several market days, been a meeting place for settlers at times of special news or events, and borne witness to all the most important happenings in Buenos Aires.

In the centre of the square can be seen the **Pirámide de Mayo**, a monument (in the form of a pyramid)

The Casa Rosada: Plaza de Mayo façade.

of great significance for Argentinians. This obelisk, topped with a sculpture representing The Republic, is known as «Altar of the Fatherland». It was decided to erect the monument, originally sited opposite the Chapter House, in 1811 to celebrate the first anniversary of the May Revolution when what had been the River Plate Vice Royalty became independent of the Spanish crown. When «La Recova» in the centre of the square was destroyed, it was decided to move the Pyramid to take its place (1912).

This monument has witnessed and symbolised many historic events: revolutions, coups d'état, restorations of democracy and political and workers' demonstrations. During the last military dictatorship which governed the country between 1976 and 1983, this was the meeting place of the «Mothers of the Plaza de Mayo», the mothers that marched in silence to reclaim their «missing» sons and daughters. Their emblem is a white headscarf.

All around the Plaza de Mayo are buildings of historical and artistic significance. Occupying land that in olden days bordered the river is the present-day Government House, better known as the **Casa Rosada** due to the pink colour it has traditionally been painted. It is the seat of the country's Executive Power, and therefore of the President. The site was formerly occupied by the Fort of Buenos Aires, at one time known as the «Royal Fortress of San Juan Baltasar de Austria». The present building brings together various structures built at different times in the site's history. In 1853, for example, part of the old fortress was demolished; in 1873 the then President Domingo F.

Several views of the Casa Rosada: balcony, detail of the coping stone of the rear façade, rear façade and patio.

AQUI DESCANSAN
LOS RESTOS
DEL CAPITAN GENERAL
D JOSE DE SAN MARTIN
Y DEL
SOLDADO DESCONOCIDO
DE LA INDEPENDENCIA
¡SALUDALOS!

Soldiers of the Regiment of Grenadiers.

Sarmiento built the left wing, to be occupied by the Post Office and Telegraphs Service; and in 1882 President Julio A. Roca gave over the other end of the building for use as the headquarters of national government. Between the two palaces there used to be a wide passageway uniting the Plaza de Mayo with a building housing the Customs Office. The archway constructed in 1894 that crosses this and unites the two wings was the work of several different hands. This is why, if you study the building carefully, you can identify three different architectural styles.

The soldiers posted in the central gateway belong to the mounted regiment known as the Regimiento de Granaderos a Caballo General José de San Martín, and form the personal escort of the President of the Republic. The balcony on its upper floor, as well as being the scenario for popular events during different presidencies, achieved importance during the mandate of Juan Domingo Perón. It was from here that many speeches, including those of his wife, Eva Duarte de Perón, were given. When the film «Evita», starring Madonna, was being shot, permission was given to film one scene on this very balcony.

Historians have never been able to discover the real reasons behind the colour of the Casa Rosada, although the most popular version recounts that the original pink tone was the result of combining whitewash and cow's blood, with the intention of giving a special colour to such a special building.

Three great buildings dominate the space on the other side of the Plaza de Mayo. The first is the **Buenos Aires Metropolitan Cathedral**. Starting its days as a simple clay and straw construction, there have been continuous efforts to improve the building. First, its walls were rebuilt with brick, and its roof with Spanish tiles. Later it grew with the city and in 1882 it took on the appearance it has

Buenos Aires Metropolitan Cathedral: detail of the «Votive Lamp».

Main façade of the Buenos Aires Metropolitan Cathedral.

Town Hall.

today. Its style is clearly Neo-Classical, with twelve columns representing the Twelve Apostles sustaining a façade depicting a biblical scene: Joseph meeting his father. The frieze is the work of the French artist José Dubourdie. Also on this façade is a «Votive Lamp», a homage to the «Liberator» General José de San Martín and to the Unknown Soldier of the Independence.

Inside the Cathedral has five wide naves, and the Great Altar, modified several times, possesses some splendid carvings and seating. One of the side naves leads to the Mausoleum of General José de San Martín, who died in France in 1850. In accordance with his wishes, his remains were repatriated and buried in this chapel, constructed for

the purpose. Resting next to this Liberator of three American countries (Argentina, Chile and Peru) are the mortal remains of General Juan Gregorio de las Heras, General Tomás Guido and the Unknown Soldier of the Independence.

The second great building is the **Town Hall of the Autonomous City of Buenos Aires**, seat of the Executive Power and therefore seat of the communal Head of Government and built between 1891 and 1902 by the engineer Juan María Cagnoni to a plan by Juan Antonio Buschiazzo. This palace combines elements from different European styles: façade in Italian neo-renaissance, sections recalling German architecture and mansards and coping stones in the French style. Its façade giving onto the Plaza de Mayo has a dome with a tower and a clock.

The last building is the **City Chapter House (Cabildo)**. This building is of great traditional significance, and has been declared a National Historical Monument. The institution of Spanish origin known as «cabildo» was an attempt to involve popular participation in decisions in early colonial times. This was where the prominent residents met to carry out the functions of the Town Hall. They had competencies over matters of education, cleaning, prisons, police, supplies, building, the deceased, etc. Starting off as a somewhat precarious construction, it was gradually improved to incorporate hard woods, tiled roofs, brick walls and ornamentation. In 1725, the Jesuit architect

City Chapter House: frontage and details of the arcades and tower.

Diagonal Norte and the Obelisk.

Avenida de Mayo.

Andrés Blanqui designed the new building, of which very little can be seen today. The original had eleven arches on its two floors, of which only five remain: three were demolished to allow the Avenida de Mayo to be widened (1889) and another three for the widening of Diagonal Sur (1931). The current building, housing the **History Museum of the Chapter House and the May Revolution**, has a double arcade, a two-storied tower and clock, a large vestibule and the Chapter Room with shields and furniture dating from the Spanish era.

From the Plaza de Mayo, looking out towards the Chapter House, there is an interesting view of three of the city's most unusual thoroughfares. To the right and left lie the only two diagonal streets of Buenos Aires. The first is known as **Diagonal Sur «Julio A. Roca»**, and along its route are located several important public buildings, such as the City Legislature (Deliberating Council) building, several ministries and government offices. The second, **Diagonal Norte «President Roque Sáenz Peña»**, was widened to join the Plaza de Mayo with the area of the Obelisk, and make it more spacious.

Between these two diagonals is a wide street with its own particular features: **Avenida de Mayo**. This traditional and attractive street was opened on 9 July 1894, during the term as Mayor of Torcuato

*Details of two
buildings on
Avenida de Mayo.*

*Avenida de Mayo
and, in the
background, the
Congress building.*

Café Tortoni: entrance and interior.

de Alvear, who decided to establish a link between the Plaza de Mayo and what was to be the National Congress. The idea was ahead of its time and required the compulsory purchase and demolition of many buildings belonging to Buenos Aires high society. Its inauguration meant the city's definitive entry into modern times, leaving behind it the era of the «Big Village». Avenida de Mayo became a favourite with the Spanish community. In its various theatres, the zarzuela reigned supreme, while in some of its cafés you could order your «drinking chocolate with fritters» «Madrid-style». Today, it still has its imposing view, majestic buildings (many of which were restored by the Spanish Crown to commemorate the 500th anniversary of the Discovery of America), traditional cafes and colourful processions for carnival. But more importantly, it is the route chosen by Presidents on the day they come into power to go from the Government House to Congress, to present their respects to the people.

Amongst its cafes is the **Café Tortoni**, one of the oldest and finest establishments in the city. Its traditional decoration combines wood, brass and mirrors. It was the meeting place of such legendary figures as Carlos Gardel, Jorge Luis Borges, Alfonsina Storni, Benito Quinquela Martín, Baldomero Fernández Moreno and Juan de Dios Filiberto, among others. These days, it offers all the romanticism of days gone by while also promoting the tango and the history of the city.

Following this avenue towards the Plaza de Los Dos Congresos you can enjoy literally dozens of buildings crammed with architectural riches, outstanding among which are number 567, formerly owned by the newspaper **La Prensa**; number 1,212, the **Avenida Theatre**, once the a venue for important Spanish theatre companies, burnt down in 1979 and reconstructed in 1994; number 1,297, the **Hotel Chile**, a fine example of the Art Nouveau style, and lastly, number 1,370, the **Pasaje Barolo**, of imposing design and for a long time the highest building in the city.

And along with all this beauty above ground, under the avenue runs what was the first metro in South America. Opened in 1911, it was constructed using

The Pasaje Barolo building.

The Hotel Chile and one of the entrances of the «A» line underground on the Avenida de Mayo.

Plaza de Los Dos Congresos.

the «open cast» method and it was one of the wonders of engineering of its time. It should be remarked that even today some of its old wooden carriages are still running, a lasting tribute to public passenger transport.

Once at the end of the Avenida de Mayo the road opens out into the **Plaza de Los Dos Congresos**. This pretty green space framed by its imposing buildings contains some notable monuments: the **Monolith of Kilometer 0**, the point of origin of all roads in the country; a copy of the sculpture **«The Thinker»** by Auguste Rodin; and the great **Monument to the Two Congresses**. The latter monument commemorates the congresses of 1813 (the assembly that established the bases of the national system) and 1816 (when independence

Sculpture «The Thinker», copy of sculpture of the same name by Auguste Rodin.

Two details of the Monument to the Two Congresses.

Front of the Monument to the Two Congresses.

The National Congress. ▷

was declared). This sculptural work by Jules Lagae, of Belgian extraction, was inaugurated in 1914. Three stairways lead to an esplanade where pride of place is given to the sculpture **«La República»** (The Republic). Behind it, another sculpture represents work, while in front there is a fanciful sculpture with an adolescent driving a foursome of spirited horses. A fountain, mingling light effects with its water, is the finishing touch before we reach the sumptuous building of the **National Congress**.

When it was decided at the end of the 19th century to build the National Congress, a nation-wide competition was announced. The winner was the Italian architect Víctor Meano. Because the building had to be ready for the celebration of the first centenary of the May Revolution –1910– it was inaugurated before completion, in 1906. Although the dominant lines of its exterior are Neo-Greco-Roman, it draws its inspiration from a palace in Berlin, while its fine dome was modelled on a tower in Turin. Its grey granite base supports columns with Corinthian capitals. A wide stairway leads to a peristyle with six columns supporting a triangular pediment. It is crowned by a bronze sculpture, work of the Italian sculptor Víctor de Pol, showing four horses being driven by «La República». Inside the building the most outstanding features are the semi-circular room housing the Deputies' Chamber, the library and the «Room of the lost steps», with its sumptuous decoration. Today this building is the seat of the country's Legislative Power, consisting of one Chamber of Senators and another of Deputies.

Dome and two details of the National Congress building.

Main façade of the National Congress.

Avenida Paseo Colón.

THE SOUTH: THE DISTRICTS OF SAN TELMO AND LA BOCA

Starting from the southern end of the Plaza de Mayo and taking the Avenida Paseo Colón, location of several buildings belonging to Ministries and military and government offices, we come to the south of the city. Two of its districts best illustrate its special attraction: San Telmo and La Boca, each with its own particular characteristics, but both with a long history and rich in tradition.

But before entering the first of these districts, we pass an important building in the **Avenida Paseo Colón**. This is the present home of the **Faculty of Engineering of the National University of Buenos Aires**, built during the second presiden-

cy of General Juan Domingo Perón. As well as its imposing presence and architectural richness, it has two curious features: the first is that there is an identical building in the northern part of the city, and the second is that it was destined to be the headquarters of the Workers' Centre (although it was never used by this body and was finally given over to the Eva Perón Foundation), while the other building in its turn became headquarters of the Businessmen's' Centre (the two political sectors that most closely defined the activity of the Perón era).

Opposite the Faculty is a monument created by a well-known Argentine sculptor: Rogelio Yrurtia. Its title is «**Song to work**» and it represents a group of 14 naked figures in two groups, one known as

Details of the sculpture «Song to Work», by Rogelio Yrurtia.

«Common Effort» and the other as «Triumph». Both are dragging a heavy stone, and guided by the strength and hope of a female figure.

To enter the district of **San Telmo** is to go back in time to the origins of the city. As the only way of getting from the centre (the Plaza Mayor) to the port, then near the present district of La Boca, San Telmo is intimately linked to the city's history. And so all along the road that is today known as Defensa Street, shops were established and private houses built. The heart of the district is **Plaza Dorrego**, formerly known as «stopping-place for carts» since it was here that all traffic from the port stopped before going on to the centre. Nowadays there is a Sunday antiques market in the square. This is a picturesque venue –a kind of «flea market» much in the style of Madrid's «Rastro»– where you can buy all kinds of antiques,

Faculty of Engineering.

Several views of the Antiques Fair held in the Plaza Dorrego every Sunday.

Church of San Telmo or Nuestra Señora de Belén: main façade and detail of the domes.

from sculptures and silverware to clothes, books and records.

The district took its name from the neighbouring church, **Nuestra Señora de Belén**, a few metres away from Plaza Dorrego in Humberto I Street. In 1806 the parish of San Telmo was founded. Over the years the area and the church itself adopted the name of the saint, really not a «Saint» at all, but a «Lay sister», to whom sailors prayed in times of need. Until the end of the 19th Century this ancient district was inhabited by the best-known families of Buenos Aires. However, in 1871 the city suffered an epidemic of yellow fever, which decimated its population. The richer families began to move north and westwards. And after the epidemic, the grand residencies where they had lived were rented out by the room to the immigrants that were by then pouring into the country. These

Caserón de la Ezeiza.

The «Casa Mínima».

beautiful and noble houses became «Conventillos» (tenements): lodgings for the most humble of these foreigners and a mixing pot of races, languages, religions and customs. These days the district is recognised as the historical centre of the city, and contains many restaurants, nightspots where you can listen to and dance the tango, antique shops and art galleries.

The Church of San Telmo (Nuestra Señora de Belén) rewards a closer study. Belonging to the order of San Ignacio de Loyola, it was commissioned from the religious architect Andrés Blanqui in 1734. But with the expulsion of the Jesuits from America by King Carlos III, the work could not be finished and it was completed in 1813, almost a

century later. In the Baroque style, in its sacristy is a white marble table that was used to treat the injured during the English invasions of the city (in 1806 and 1807).

Another building of interest as an example of the former «conventillos» is the house known today as the **Caserón de la Ezeiza**. At number 1,179 of Defensa Street, it was built in 1880 in a quasi-Italian style, almost in the style of a Roman house, with a large intricately worked iron gate and three patios (reflecting the practices of the time: one for the family, one for the servants and the third as a stable, vegetable garden and coach house). This building had several uses in its long life: as a family home, a school and finally a «conventillo» housing in its day up to one hundred souls. The tenants were re-housed in 1980; the building was rehabilitated, and it has a new life as a pleasant shopping and antiques gallery.

You cannot leave the centre of this district without viewing one of the curiosities of Buenos Aires: the «Casa Mínima» at number 380, pasaje San Lorenzo. This unusual house has a façade only 2.17 metres wide. It does not seem possible that such a small plot should have been chosen for building a house, but in fact it was the result of a bad distribution of land leading to the existence of this tiny and almost unusable site, only big enough for a door and a hallway.

To stroll through San Telmo, following its narrow, twisting little streets, past its old houses and its nostalgic cafes, lets you recreate the Buenos Aires of yesteryear, when the city was still just a small settlement on a village scale.

Returning to Avenida Paseo Colón and continuing southwards, we come to **Lezama Park**. This includes one of the few natural ravines preserved in the city, giving strength to the theory that claims the earliest origins of Buenos Aires lie here. In this leafy wooded park are several sculptures and the old villa of the Lezama family that nowadays houses the **Museum of National History**. A striking feature along one side of the park is the **Russian Orthodox Church**, a reproduction of the church in Moscow's Red Square.

The San Telmo district.

Several views of the San Telmo district.

51

A corner of Lezama Park.

Lezama Park: Russian Orthodox Church. ▷

Lezama Park: Museum of National History.

Lezama Park: Vantage point.

Continuing southwards, you enter the district of **La Boca**, a picturesque sector of the city crammed with history, legends and beautiful nooks and crannies. This was the site of the old port of Buenos Aires, and it takes its name from the **Boca del Riachuelo**, or the mouth of the small river Riachuelo, running into the River Plate. Originally this was low ground with banana trees, abundant vegetation and indigenous animals. Around the middle of the nineteenth century immigrants of Italian origin began to arrive, particularly from Genoa and Sicily. These immigrants were sailors or port workers, and they chose to set up home in this sector of the city, giving the area its special character. Since this was low-lying land affected several times a year by the Riachuelo bursting its banks, its settlers did not build their houses to last, but used materials such as wood, zinc sheeting and even sometimes material from the boats in which they worked. It is said that the practice of painting the fronts of the houses in several colours is due to the paint coming from the boats being repaired in the port. All this gives the district a characteristic appearance whose tradition lives on today.

Over the years, the district of La Boca has became one of the centres of the city's tourism. Its interest includes its houses with their colourful frontages: although apparently very humble they are comfortably equipped inside; and the River Riachuelo itself, still contaminated and foul-smelling, crossed by two bridges: the older made of iron and the more recent of concrete; and finally the «boteros» or ferries, transporting passengers from bank to bank for a couple of centavos.

Aerial view of Puerto Madero and the port (by courtesy of Diario La Nación).

Typical houses in the La Boca district.

Striped boat in the mouth of the Riachuelo.

La Boca: the two bridges crossing the Riachuelo.

58

Main frontage of the Pedro de Mendoza Municipal School, site of the Museum dedicated to Benito Quinquela Martín, and a view of the picturesque Caminito Street.

Right in the centre of La Boca we find **Caminito Street**, immortalised by a tango composed by Juan de Dios Filiberto. Caminito Street was once a shallow stream, then until 1920 it served as a railway line, and finally a path and a rubbish tip. And although the tango pre-dates today's picturesque street, its names have attained fame together. Today it is the setting for artistic activities (painting and sculpture) and is frequented by travelling salesmen, making it a kind of open-air museum and theatre, a theatre without doors that is virtually unique of its kind in the world.

Only a step away is the **Museum and Studio of Benito Quinquela Martín**, the famous Argentine artist whose work is full of views of the port and the district. His impressionist palette, loaded with colours and bearing the traces of vigorous working with a spatula, make this painter's work a kind of animated sample of the life in the port, the work of the men who seek their living at sea and the subtle tonalities that the different times of day and the seasons give to this part of the city. Both the Museum and the Studio are located above the **Pedro de Mendoza Municipal School**. Benito Quinquela Martín (1890-1977) is one of Argentina's best-known painters. A popular philosopher, a loveable bohemian, he took part in every cultural movement of the city between 1930 and 1950.

Taking Avenida Paseo Colón and continuing by

Perspective of the passageway through the Puerto Madero.

Ingeniero Huergo, we reach the port known as **Puerto Madero**. When the city grew larger and its first port was no longer big enough, plans were made to build a new one, more suited to larger keeled and better-equipped ships. Of two projects originally presented, the idea of Eduardo Madero won the day: an «English style» port opposite the city, with locks, swing bridges, four jetties and two docks. The work finished in 1897 and large warehouses built on its banks in the English style with English materials. These new installations at once became inadequate, and it was decided to extend them northwards. This forms what is today known as Puerto Nuevo (the New Port), work on which finished in 1926. In time, Puerto Madero with its large warehouses was no longer serviceable, and it fell into disuse. It is a curious fact that a city

whose inhabitants call themselves «porteños» (from the word port) have in real life turned their backs both on the river and on the port itself. For decades, under military administration, access to these areas was restricted. But in 1989 it was decided to recover this space for the city: not only were its buildings rehabilitated, but a new district «looking to the river» was developed. And so the «Puerto Madero District» came into being, which is today a beautiful promenade that houses in its rehabilitated warehouses: restaurants, offices, homes, quays and jetties, hotels and the headquarters of Argentina's Catholic University. Its streets bear the names of famous women, it has a tourist train running all round it, and, particulary on Sundays, it is a favourite place for a stroll amongst visitors and inhabitants alike.

Leisure complex, cranes and an old warehouse building.

«Las Catalinas».

THE NORTH: «LAS CATALINAS» AND THE DISTRICTS OF EL RETIRO, LA RECOLETA AND PALERMO

Looking northwards from Puerto Madero, you can already catch a glimpse of the area known as **Catalinas Norte** or simply «Las Catalinas». Although this part of the city has a history going back to the beginning of the 18th Century, it took on particular importance two centuries later, in 1970. The subsoil of this small number of plots is one of the few containing the volcanic rock tuffa, permitting the construction of buildings of great height and imposing presence. And this explains why, after a first experiment in the form of the **Hotel Sheraton** which opened in 1972, several multinational companies sited their offices in this sector of the city. The style they chose was for the most part that of the School of Chicago –steel and glass– giving the district a futurist and stylish air. Practically all its buildings are «intelligent», that is, with their systems of security, air conditioning, lighting and maintenance controlled electronically. One of the latest and most unusual in design is the **República Building**, the work of the world-renowned Argentine architect César Pelli.

Next to «Las Catalinas» and going northwards we enter the district of **El Retiro** (the Retreat), formerly a coastal suburb of the city. Inhabitants valued this high region, with its cliffs overlooking the river, and constructed country villas there. Its name comes from the hermitage (of San Sebastián) which formerly occupied the site, and in which people could engage in «retreats» for spiritual reasons or simply take a rest.

Sheraton Hotel.

A view of «Las Catalinas» and the Republica Building.

63

Monument to the fallen in the Falklands War.

Monument to General San Martín. ▷

In its long history this area has also been a slave enclave, a military training ground, a bull ring and lastly, when the yellow fever epidemic devastated the south of the city, it became the place chosen by richer families to build their new villas, many of which can still be seen today. The centre of the district is formed by two very different but equally important squares: the Plaza San Martín and the Plaza Fuerza Aérea.

The **Plaza San Martín** has a pronounced raised area, ending in two monuments of historical relevance both for the city and for the country. One is dedicated to **General José de San Martín**, the Father of the Nation. It was erected in 1862, later modified, and its red granite base supports the equestrian statue of the Liberator. To complete this monument, the site where homage is paid to

official visitors to the country, there are several base-reliefs and sculptural groups.

The second monument is dedicated «**To the Fallen in the War of the Islands of Malvinas and the Southern Atlantic**». In this cenotaph erected in 1983 are displayed granite plaques with the names of the 650 Argentine soldiers killed in the war for the sovereignty of the Falklands (or Malvinas) Islands. Around the square are located fine palaces dating from the turn of the 20th Century, currently occupied by official organisations, hotels and offices. Notable is the residence of the Anchorena family, today known as the **San Martín Palace**, the headquarters of the Argentina Chancellery; the Palace of the Paz family, incorporating some ideas taken from the Louvre in Paris and completed in 1914, today headquarters of the **Military Circle**,

65

Two views of the gardens in the Plaza San Martín.

San Martín Palace, present-day HQ of the Argentine Chancellor's office.

The former Palace of the Paz family, now HQ of the Military Circle.

The Kavanagh building.

The Retiro railway station.

and the **Plaza Hotel**, opened in 1909, which has accommodated personalities such as the Shah of Persia, Charles de Gaulle, Indira Ghandi, Theodore Roosevelt, Prince Philip, Duke of Edinburgh, the King and Queen of Spain and Neil Armstrong, among other notable visitors to the city.

One last building which, although not very old, still deserves to be mentioned, is the **Kavanagh Building**. With its rigid lines, this exponent of the «monumentalist» style used for housing won various national and international prizes, the most outstanding of which was that awarded by the American Society Of Civil Engineers: «International historical milestone of Engineering» (1994), and was for several decades the highest building in the city.

Opposite the Plaza San Martín is the **Plaza Fuerza**

Aérea, formerly called «Britania» since it contains a replica of the tower of London. It is popularly known as the **Tower of the English**. Around this square two large constructions stand out: the **Hotel Sheraton** and the **Retiro Railway Station**. This last is in fact a complex of three stations and the starting point of the suburban and intercity lines leading to the north and northwest of Argentina. Twenty years ago a new and very modern addition was made, to act as the terminus for all intercity passenger coach movements: the **Buenos Aires Bus Station**.

Between these two squares we find the start of **Avenida del Libertador General San Martín**, one of the most important and finest thoroughfares in Buenos Aires and the main highway towards the north of the city. Although spacious here, along

Two views of the Buenos Aires Bus Station, and a view of the Plaza Fuerza Aérea with the Tower of the English.

The Patio Bullrich, in the Avenida del Libertador.

Avenida del Libertador, centre.

70

The Prourban building.

its nearly 20 kilometres it takes on different names and varies in appearance.

Crossing the Avenida del Libertador towards the districts of la Recoleta and Palermo, we see some buildings that attract our interest. At number 700 is the **Patio Bullrich** shopping centre, a complex built over the structure of a traditional seconds shop that these days includes shops dedicated to the sale of the major international brands, restaurants, cafeterias and cinemas. Due to its position near many large hotels, this centre is one of the most visited by tourists.

At number 1,000 is an unusual building, the **Prourban**, popularly known as «El Rulero» (The roller), a circular construction occupied by offices, and work of the architects Manteola, Sánchez Gómez, Santos and Solsona.

Opposite the Prourban is the **Park Hyatt Hotel**. This was put up in 1992 on land formerly housing the residence of the Alzaga Unzué family. Since the old palace was subject to a conservation order that meant it could not be demolished, the hotel had to incorporate it into its new structure. And so the rooms of the old building today form the lounges of the new.

Above this avenue and from number 1,900 onwards lies the **Carlos Thays Park**, one of the most recently created parks in the city, and extending for more than a kilometre. This park was built on public land and other terrain acquired from a large amusement park, the Italpark, now almost in the centre of the city. The park's name is taken from the French architect and creator of the Botanical Gardens and many other parks in Buenos Aires, and it includes several sculptural works, the best of which is the **«Male Torso»** by the internationally renowned Colombian sculptor Fernando Botero. Around number 2,600, Avenida del Libertador runs one-way, its other half being Avenida Presidente Figueroa Alcorta. This gives access to the city's «green lung»: the Tres de Febrero Park, known as «Los Bosques de Palermo» (The woods of Palermo), and described below.

To be found at the start of the Avenida Alcorta is

Carlos Thays Park: sculpture of «Male Torso».

71

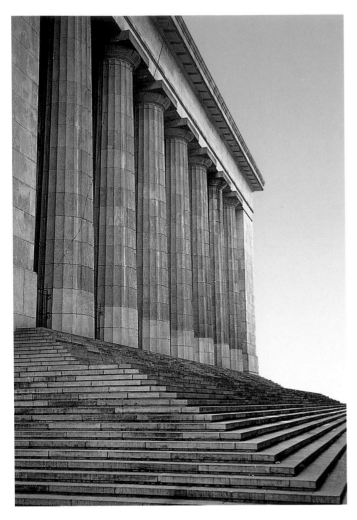

Main frontage and stairway of the Law Faculty, in the Avenida Figueroa Alcorta.

the **Law Faculty of the University of Buenos Aires**. This is the twin building to that located in the southern part of the city, built during the second term of office as President of Juan Domingo Perón. An interesting anecdote is that its stairways have recently been used for several fashion parades and musical recitals, as is the custom in some European cities.

At its intersection with Austria Street are two striking buildings. On the right, the offices of **Canal 7 Television**, built specifically for use as a television broadcasting centre. From here, in 1978, colour images were broadcast to the world of the World Cup Football Championship. It is currently the only official television channel. Opposite is the **Embassy of the Republic of Chile**, whose interest comes from the fact that it is the only diplomatic residence located in a square.

Before entering the Tres de Febrero Park, and at the junction with Avenida Sarmiento, we find the **monument to General Justo José de Urquiza**. This large red granite and bronze group is the work of the sculptors Héctor Rocha (Argentine) and Renzo Baldi (Italian). Inaugurated in 1958, it commemorates the figure of the soldier who brought the civil wars to an end after independence, and who gave the country a National Constitution (Magna Carta), which remained in force for more than a century.

When you enter the **Bosques de Palermo** you leave the big city behind and lose yourself in its more than 300 hectares of greenery. Tucked away inside this park are several artificial lakes, monuments, paths for cyclists, places you can practice sport, a rose garden, an «Andalusian Patio », the Zoo, the Botanical Gardens and the Planetarium. Its history goes back to the origins of the city. Sited on low land, it was subject to flooding due to its location at the mouth of the Maldonado River, now diverted into underground piping. Starting off as one property, it was then divided into smaller plots for second homes, until in 1874 the then President Domingo Faustino Sarmiento decided to create the Tres de Febrero Park. The existing trees, lakes and pathways were incorporated. The French landscape architect Carlos Thays was entrusted with the definitive design.

A visit to the park is not complete without exploring its many parts: the three **artificial lakes**, where you can go out in rowing boats; **The Rosegarden**, so named because it contains thousands of roses, including some rare varieties such as the black rose; the **«Andalusian Patio»**, designed with beautiful ceramic tiles donated by the City Hall of Seville (Spain); **«The Japanese Garden»**, a fenced-off area that recreates the parks of Japan; the **Planetarium**, a curious structure resembling a space ship and used as an astronomy training centre; the **Zoo**, today managed by a private company, and considered to be one of the best in the world; the **Botanical Gardens**, almost at the edge of the park; and approaching the city, the **Buenos Aires Islamic Centre and Mosque**, several military

The Bosques de Palermo: two perspectives of the Artificial Lakes.

The Bosques de Palermo: details of «The Andalusian Patio» and the «Japanese Garden».

The Bosques de Palermo: the Planetarium, the Botanical Gardens and the elephants in the Zoo.

Monument «To the Magna Carta and the Four Regions of Argentina», better known as Monument of the Spanish (by courtesy of Diario La Nación).

offices, sporting clubs and spaces for open-air leisure and sport.

Going back along Avenida del Libertador towards the centre, we find an imposing monument where it crosses Avenida Sarmiento. Although officially called **«To the Magna Carta and the Four Regions of Argentina»**, it is better known as the Monument of the Spanish, since it was a gift of the Spanish community to the city. It was opened in 1927 and consists of four large sculptural groups, representing the Argentine regions of Andes, Río de la Plata, Chaco and la Pampa, with a base on which rests the sculpture of «La Republica» with her wind-blown vestments.

Where we cross Tagle Street a building in the «monumentalist» style can be seen, in the form of the head offices of the **Argentine Automobile Club**. This was a pioneer amongst automobile clubs in the world, being only the third to be created, and today forms the centre of logistical support to its members on matters of mechanics, information, tourism, legal paperwork and insurance.

At number 1,902, housed in an imposing palace that once belonged to the Errazuri family, is the **National Museum of Decorative Art**. This fine building conceals within it invaluable works of art, outstanding among which are Flemish tapestries, furniture from many different eras and styles, silverware, marble, etc.

Reaching Austria Street, we find the **National Libary,** opened in 1991, that gives room to approximately three and a half million books. It took almost twenty years to build and suffered many interruptions. Important features are its «Treasures Room», for keeping old and irreplaceable works, an auditorium with a capacity of 300, an Exhibitions

National Museum of Decorative Art.

National Library.

Monument to Eva Duarte de Perón.

Room and rooms for multimedia, music and the Braille system.

Opposite the Library and only recently opened is the **Monument to María Eva Duarte de Perón (Evita)**. Evita is commemorated for her fight for the rights of the poor and women.

Near the Library and before we reach the district of la Recoleta is the **Fine Arts Museum**. This museum, originally split amongst several organisations, was created in 1895. In 1931 it was assigned its present building which had originally housed the system for pumping the city water and which was in disuse. Due to the sheer number (approximately 15,000), quality and fame of the works of art found here it is considered one of the most important museums in America, and indeed in the world. It has the largest collection of works by Argentine artists, among them Carlos Morel, Prilidiano Pueyrredón, Carlos Enrique Pellegrini, Ernesto de la Cárcova, Lino Spilimbergo, Benito Quinquela Martín, Fernando Fader, Eduardo Sívori, Raúl Soldi, Antonio Berni, Raquel Forner and Emilio Pettoruti, to name but a few. The museum also has an important specialist library, restoration workshops and conference rooms, and is in continuous use for interesting temporary exhibitions.

After leaving Avenida Pueyrredón we come to the district of **La Recoleta**. At the end of the 18th Century this was uninhabited countryside, far outside the city centre. Its name refers to the presence in the area of «reclusive monks» (monjes recoletos) belonging to the Franciscan Order. Around the mid 18th Century these monks had built a monastery on ground they had been given, thus lending their name to the district.

These days this sector of the city is one of the best-developed areas for both daytime and after-dark entertainment. Numerous restaurants, discotheques, shops of well-known brands, the Buenos Aires Hard Rock Café, Buenos Aires Design (a shopping centre devoted to decoration) and an imposing recently-opened cinema complex, Village Cines Recoleta, with more than ten high-tech cinemas, all make for an offer that attracts a huge public, above all at weekends.

The centre of the district is the **Church of la Pilar**.

MUSEO NACIONAL DE BELLAS ARTES

National Fine Arts Museum.

The district of La Recoleta.

*The district of
La Recoleta.*

District of La Recoleta: detail of Recoleta Village and Avenida Quintana.

This church has been a basilica since 1934 and is a National Historical Monument. It is one of the most typical vestiges of the colonial period, and an example of Jesuitical architecture. A simple façade with a single, square-based tower and bell-tower, with no baroque elements, in keeping with its very austere religious order. Its original construction dates from 1732, although over the years it has undergone several rehabilitations and restorations. Inside it has a single central nave with several chapels with carvings and images from the 18th Century, even including some of Peruvian origin.

To the left of the church is the **La Recoleta Cemetery**. These days almost just a place for taking a stroll, it is set on the former «holy ground» of the Church of la Pilar. In 1822 the land was confiscated from the monks and designated as the official Cemetery for the Northern Area (public and Catholic). Here are laid to rest the majority of the illustrious figures from the country's political, military, cultural and ecclesiastical past.

Details of the bell tower and the steeple of the Church of la Pilar.

Frontage of the Church of la Pilar.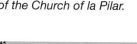

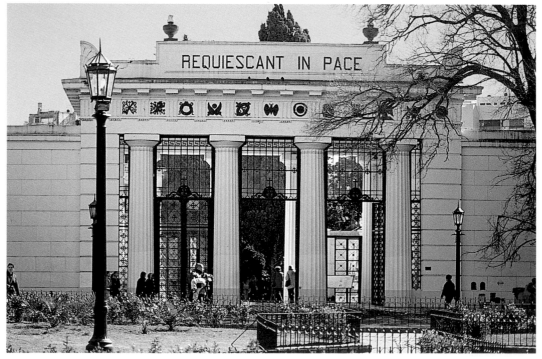

*La Recoleta
Cemetery:
mausoleums and
entry gate.*

Details of the mausoleum of Eva Perón.

Traditional and economically powerful families also have their vaults here. Many of these have interesting architectural designs, and are richly ornamented with sculptured figures.

To the right of the church is the **Recoleta Cultural Centre**. Originally the site of the Convent of the same name, after its confiscation from the monks it has had various uses: hospital, prison, military barracks, Beggars' Asylum and lastly, a residence for senior citizens. It was then decided to recycle the building and convert into a cultural centre. Now its rooms, with their views over the old patios of the former convent, are used for temporary exhibitions of painting, photography, sculpture, etc. The former chapel is now an auditorium where concerts, generally of baroque or chamber music, are held. This cultural centre tries to promote the activities of young or new artists, giving them exhibition space to promote their work.

La Recoleta Cultural Centre.

Auditorium of the La Recoleta Cultural Centre.

Street of the La Recoleta Cultural Centre.

On Sundays in the square that forms such a perfect backdrop for the Cemetery, the Church and the Cultural Centre, exhibitions of popular artists attract crowds of visitors.

In 1990 the part of the old convent that was in the worst state of repair was conceded for the construction of a shopping centre and restaurants. This is the present **Buenos Aires Design**, judged to be the best enterprise of its type in the world by a jury of the International Federation of Real Estate Professionals of Paris, in 1995.

On Saturdays, Sundays and holidays a **Craft Fair** is held in the sloping ground at one side of the shopping complex. This is one of the oldest and biggest fairs in the city.

Returning to the city centre city via Avenida Presidente Alvear, one's attention is drawn by the French-styled villas that are built along the entire length of the street. Some are particularly interesting: the **Palacio de la Nunciatura** at number 1,637, the offices of the **National Cultural Secretariat** at number 1,600, the **Alvear Palace Hotel** (built in 1932 and the favourite venue of Buenos Aires high society for holding its major celebrations) and, lastly, a small square housing the buildings of the **Jockey Club**, the **Embassy of the Federal Republic of Brazil** and the **French Embassy**. We only need to go round this villa to come out into Avenida 9 de Julio, and a little further on, to come back to the starting point of this tour.

Two views of the Craft Fair held in Plaza Francia on weekends and holidays.

Abasto Buenos Aires Shopping: façade and interior.

Buenos Aires shopping

The city is an excellent space for «shopping trips». «Porteños» are great lovers of elegance, culture, fun and good food. As well as the products that have always distinguished national industry for their quality and good taste –leathers, skins and high fashion– a policy of extensive importation has filled shop windows with goods from the widest variety of brands and countries throughout the world. Even today the traditional shopping streets are lined with enterprises that excel in the presentation of their products. In recent years a large number of Shopping Centres have been built all over Buenos Aires, these are commonly known as «Shoppings». The majority are large structures on several floors with shops, cinemas, exhibition areas and spaces dedicated to gastronomy known as «Patios de Comidas» (Food Halls).

Some of these must be mentioned simply because their design and decoration justify a visit: the **Alto Palermo Shopping** (Avenida Santa Fe/Coronel Díaz), in the Norte district with its large number of clients, in general young people; the **Patio Bullrich** (Avenida del Libertador/Montevideo) near the large hotels and with an excellent choice of world famous brands; the **Galerías Pacífico** (Avenida Córdoba/Florida), right in the centre and of architectural interest, and the **Abasto Buenos Aires Shopping** (Avenida Corrientes/Agüero), one of the most recently opened, making use of one of the city's former fruit and vegetable warehouses.

Two views of Alto Palermo Shopping, interior of Patio Bullrich and Galerías Pacífico.

Book Fair.

Detail of the exhibition «Arte BA».

Buenos Aires at night

The «porteño» has always loved the night, and the city's response to his demands is a wide range of entertainment: concerts, opera, ballet, theatre, cinema, musical recitals and discotheques.

The greatest number of these is concentrated at weekends, when between cinemas and theatres, the entertainments sections of the Press may offer more than 400 alternatives. There is something for all tastes, ages and budgets.

Cinemas hold continuous projections starting at mid-day and going on past mid-night.

Theatres, in general, offer one function on week-days and two on Fridays and Saturdays, usually at nine and eleven in the evening.

And discotheques open until well into the following morning, usually till after three.

Another important feature is that throughout the year, although particularly in the summer period, a lot of open-air and free entertainment is provided by official bodies.

Buenos Aires, art and exhibitions

In addition to its museums, of which the city has more than fifty, there is a large number of art galleries showing the works of both Argentine and foreign artists.

A study of the cultural agenda will enable you to visit special displays, some international touring exhibitions and others of local origin, both guaranteeing the visitor the highest levels of creativity and quality.

In recent years «Arte BA», which brings together new and established artists, has grown in prominence.

Throughout the year Buenos Aires holds exhibitions in its many facilities provided for the purpose. These cover the most diverse of subjects, although outstanding for its tradition, its sheer number of visitors and its international renown is the event known as the «Book Fair –Buenos Aires– from Author to Reader», visited each year by more than a million people, and the «Rural Argentina Show», an exhibition of farming, agriculture and industry now in its 100th showing.

Aerial view of the city showing Avenida Nueve de Julio going south (by courtesy of Diario La Nación).

Aerial view of the River Plate football field (by courtesy of Diario La Nación).

By way of goodbye

Buenos Aires, a city rich in architecture, history and art, with its fine avenues, its traditionally rushed inhabitants, its personalities in the windows of its cafés. A city with an aftertaste of Paris, Madrid and New York. A metropolis almost on the edge of the world, invoking great affection in its natives and its visitors alike. And faced with the sad task of leaving it and the hope of coming back one day, what better than to recall the fine verses written by Alfredo Le Pera for the song «Mi Buenos Aires Querido», performed by Carlos Gardel:

«My beloved Buenos Aires, when I see you again, there will be no more sorrowor forgetting...

Today luck wants me to see you again, Porteño city of my only love, and I hear the lament of a bandoneón asking for his heart to be set free».

Details of Buenos Aires.

CONTENTS

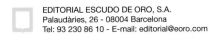

EDITORIAL ESCUDO DE ORO, S.A.
Palaudàries, 26 - 08004 Barcelona
Tel: 93 230 86 10 - E-mail: editorial@eoro.com

I.S.B.N. 987-9473-17-5
Printed by FISA - Escudo de Oro, S.A.
Legal Dep. B. 32209-2005

Protegemos el bosque; papel procedente de cultivos forestales controlados
Wir schützen den Wald. Papier aus kontrollierten Forsten.
We protect our forests. The paper used comes from controlled forestry plantations
Nous sauvegardons la forêt: papier provenant de cultures forestières contrôlées